BIG OCEAN CREATURES

written by Mary Gribbin
illustrated by Peter Bull

Ladybird

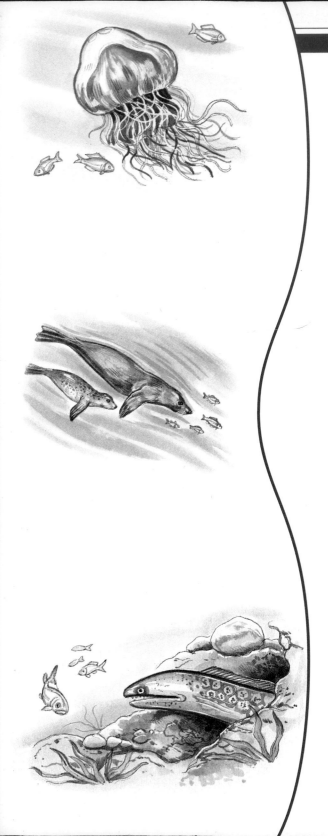

Words in **bold** are explained
in the glossary.

Originally published in the United Kingdom by
Ladybird Books Ltd 1995

First American edition by Ladybird Books,
a division of Penguin Books USA Inc.
375 Hudson Street, New York, New York 10014

Printed in the United States
10 9 8 7 6 5 4 3 2 1

ISBN 0-7214-5689-8

Contents

Blue Whale

A blue whale gulps huge mouthfuls of water. The water contains plankton and other food.

Food is trapped in the whale's mouth by the **baleen**, a curtain of strands that hangs in its mouth.

Water is forced out through the baleen. The food remains in the whale's mouth and is then swallowed.

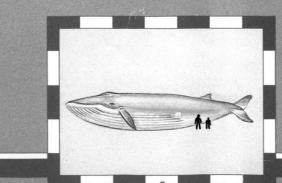

The blue whale is the largest animal that has ever lived. Like all whales, the blue whale is a **mammal**. Although it lives in the ocean, it must come to the surface to breathe. The whale breathes through the blowhole on the top of its head.

The blue whale eats **plankton** and tiny shrimplike creatures called **krill**. One whale can eat more than four tons of food a day. Whales swim by moving their powerful tails up and down. They communicate with each other by sending loud squealing noises through the water.

Whale Shark

The whale shark is the largest **fish**–and the largest shark–in the ocean. Like other fish, it breathes underwater through its **gills**. Although it has over 300 rows of tiny teeth, the whale shark does not attack or eat other large sea animals.

Like whales, it feeds on plankton. The whale shark lives in warm, tropical waters. During the day, it looks for food deep in the ocean. At night, it searches for food near the surface.

Scientists think female whale sharks lay large **fertilized** eggs on the ocean floor.

The baby whale shark grows inside the egg and feeds on the yolk.

When the baby whale shark is ready to hatch, it forces its way out of the egg.

Octopus

The octopus lives in dark holes and crevices near the ocean floor. It piles up rocks and shells in front of the hole to hide from **predators** or to lie in wait for **prey**. An octopus has a soft, boneless body and tough skin for protection. Every octopus has eight arms, or **tentacles**. If an octopus loses one of its tentacles, a new one

An octopus hides among the rocks and plants on the ocean floor waiting for prey.

An octopus can change its skin color to help it blend in with its surroundings.

If an octopus is threatened, it shoots out a stream of dark ink. The water turns black and the octopus escapes.

will grow in its place. Each tentacle is covered with hundreds of suckers. The octopus uses these suckers to break open the shells of crabs, clams, mussels, and other small **shellfish**. Then it uses its tentacles to put the food into its mouth. The octopus's mouth is underneath its head, where the tentacles meet.

When a female green turtle is ready to lay eggs, she climbs onto the shore.

She digs a deep hole into which she lays about one hundred leathery eggs.

Two months later, the baby green turtles hatch. They rush to the water and swim away.

Green Turtle

The green turtle is one of the biggest **reptiles** in the ocean. When threatened, the green turtle pulls its head and legs inside its tough, protective shell.

With its strong, paddlelike flippers, the green turtle is a powerful swimmer. It eats mainly seaweed and other plants that grow in the ocean. The female green turtle crawls onto dry land to lay her eggs.

Manta Ray

The manta ray is the biggest **ray** in the ocean. It swims near the surface with its mouth open to catch plankton, small fish, and shellfish. This huge, flat fish does not sting or bite, and it is not dangerous to humans.

A manta ray has huge side fins that look like wings.

By flapping its fins slowly up and down, a manta ray pushes itself forward through the water.

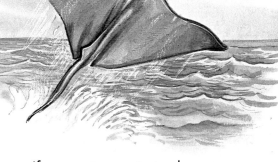

If a manta ray is in danger, it will leap up to 5 feet out of the water to escape.

A lion's mane jellyfish has poisonous tentacles that extend below its body.

The jellyfish uses its tentacles to sting and paralyze its prey.

Even when washed up on the beach, a lion's mane jellyfish can still sting.

The lion's mane jellyfish is one of the biggest jellyfish in the world. It has long, trailing tentacles underneath its large, bell-shaped body.

A jellyfish has neither a brain nor a skeleton. It moves through the ocean by pumping water in and out of its body. The jellyfish's diet includes plankton, fish, and sometimes other jellyfish. Its mouth is on the underside of the jellyfish's body.

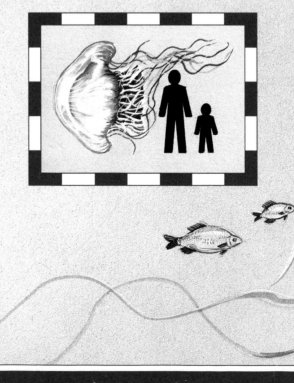

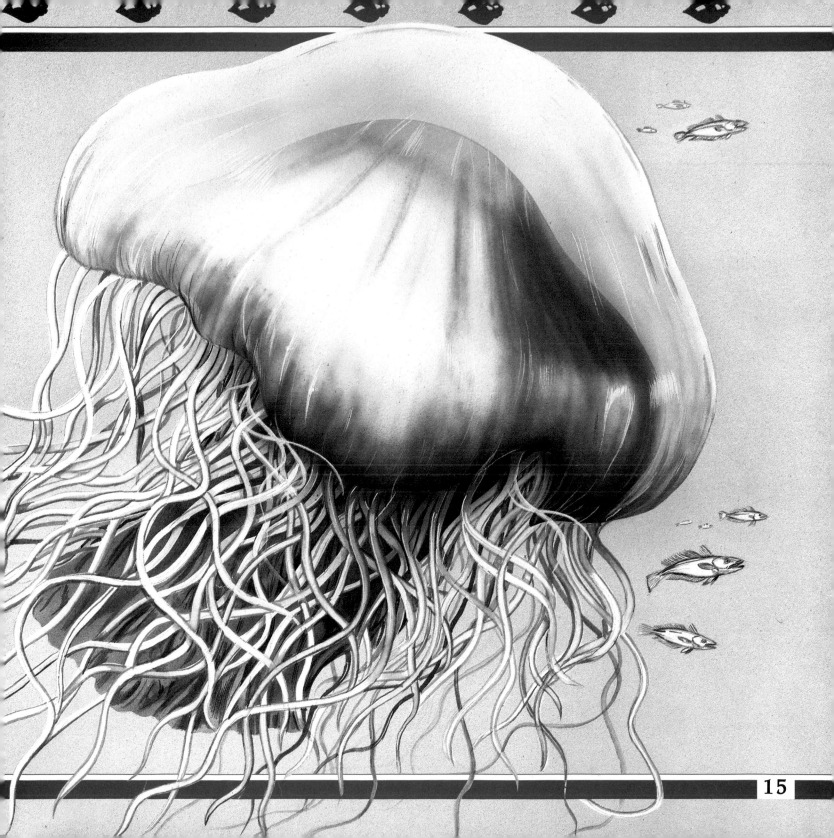

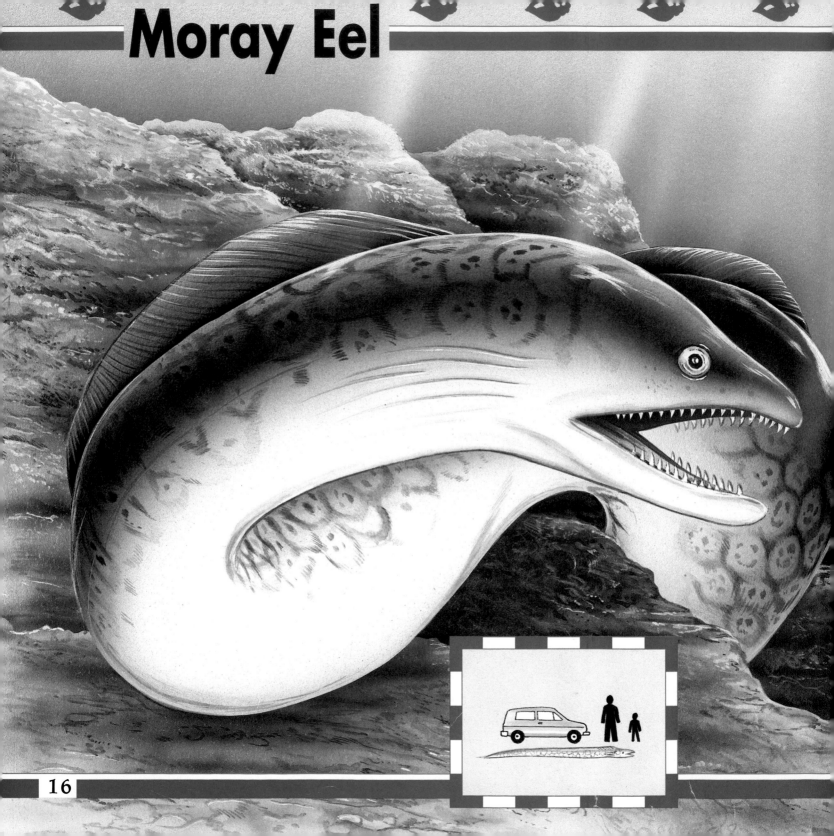

The moray eel is one of the biggest eels in the ocean. During the day, this eel **stays in** its hole on the rocky seabed. It comes out at night to hunt for food. The moray eel takes in water through its nostrils. It can smell any prey–such as fish–that are nearby.

Human divers have been bitten by moray eels.

A moray eel hides in its **lair,** waiting for fish and other prey to swim by.

The moray eel strikes quickly and grabs its victim. The eel has sharp teeth and powerful jaws.

A coral shrimp, just a few inches long, crawls into the eel's mouth and eats the leftover food.

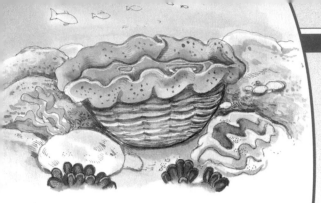

The giant clam is found on **coral reefs.** The clam grows slowly and lives for many years.

The giant clam usually stays open. Plants growing inside the clam make it appear a bright bluish green.

If a giant clam is disturbed by a diver or other intruder, it snaps shut.

Giant Clam

The giant clam is the biggest shellfish in the world. It also has the heaviest shell. The clam feeds by sucking in water and filtering tiny creatures through millions of tiny hairlike strands.

The clam is a soft-bodied animal protected by two large shells. Strong muscles open and close the shells. When the clam is threatened, it closes the two shells tightly together.

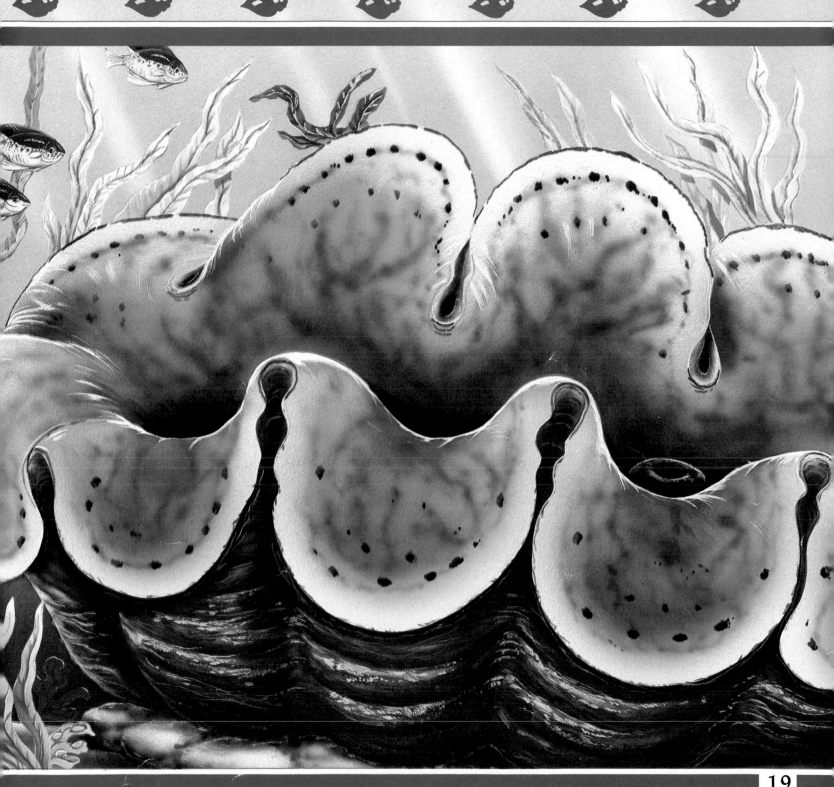

The elephant seal is the biggest seal in the ocean. It gets its name from the male elephant seal's large nose. The male elephant seal is called a bull; the female is called a cow. Cows do not have large noses and are almost ten times smaller than males.

During the mating season, the bulls often fight to prove who is the strongest. They puff up their noses to make themselves look bigger and more powerful. The bulls also roar, bellow, and rear up on their bellies to keep rivals away.

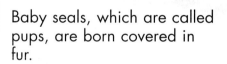

In the spring, elephant seals gather on shore in large **colonies** to breed.

Baby seals, which are called pups, are born covered in fur.

When the pups are big enough to hunt for their own food, the elephant seals return to the ocean.

Fascinating Facts

Blue Whale

The calls of the blue whale are louder than the calls of any other sea creature.

Whale Shark

Since its skin is dark on the top and light on the bottom, the whale shark blends in with its surroundings from any angle.

Octopus

The Australian blue-ringed octopus is extremely deadly. Its poisonous venom can kill a person in minutes.

Green Turtle

The female green turtle swims thousands of miles through the ocean but returns to the same beach every year to lay her eggs.

Manta Ray

The manta ray is sometimes called a devilfish because its fins look like a flapping black cloak.

Jellyfish

The Australian box jellyfish is the deadliest jellyfish in the world. Its sting can kill a person in less than 4 minutes.

Moray Eel

One type of moray eel has flat teeth instead of sharp, pointed ones. This is because it feeds on crabs, which it crushes in its mouth.

Giant Clam

Clams have the longest lifespan of all shellfish. A giant clam can live for over 100 years.

Elephant Seal

The elephant seal can stay underwater for 20 minutes before coming up for air. It can dive as deep as 2,000 feet.

Glossary

Baleen A large, curtainlike sheet that hangs in a whale's mouth. These sheets allow the whale to filter microscopic food from the water.

Colony A group of animals that live together.

Coral reef An area of hard rock under the sea, built up by the skeletons of tiny creatures.

Fertilized Eggs that have young growing inside them.

Fish A group of animals that swim and breathe in water.

Gills Organs on the side of a fish's head that allow it to breathe in water.

Krill Tiny, shrimplike creatures that are eaten in huge numbers by whales and other sea animals.

Lair The resting or hiding place of a wild animal.

Mammal An animal that gives birth to live young and feeds them on its own milk.

Plankton Tiny drifting plants and animals that live near the surface of the ocean.

Predator An animal that hunts and eats other animals.

Prey An animal that is eaten by other animals.

Ray A wide, flat fish related to the shark.

Reptile An animal that usually lays eggs and has scales on its skin.

Shellfish Creatures living in the water that are protected by shells instead of scales.

Tentacles Armlike parts of an octopus's body used to catch food.

Index

Big Giggles

Where does a 100-ton blue whale sit?
Anywhere it wants to.

What do young whale sharks eat for lunch?
Peanut butter and jellyfish sandwiches.

What hotels do green turtles stay at?
Holiday Fins

What did Cinderella's seal wear to the ball?
Glass flippers.

How do you get a manta ray on a roller coaster?
Buy him a ticket.

How do you get four moray eels in a Volkswagon?
Two in the front and two in the back.

Which ocean won the basketball game?
Neither. It was a tide.

How do baby sharks know how to swim?
Finstinct.

What do you get when you cross a jeep with a submarine?
A four-whale dive vehicle.

Who was the most wanted octopus in the Wild West?
Billy the Squid.

Comparative Sizes

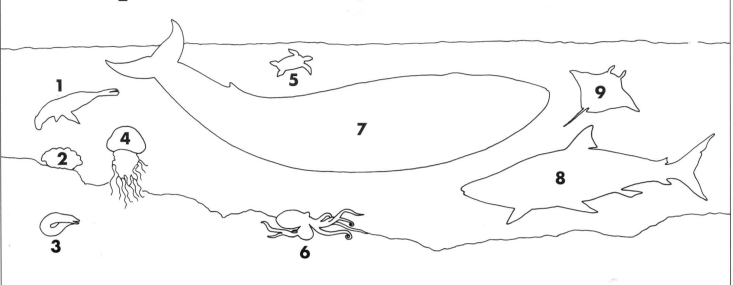

1. Elephant Seal

Some large, male elephant seals can grow to be nearly 16 feet long.

2. Giant Clam

The giant clam can be more than 3 feet across, large enough for a person to sit in.

3. Moray Eel

Some moray eels are longer than a family car.

4. Lion's Mane Jellyfish

These jellyfish have 45-foot-long tentacles.

5. Green Turtle

A green turtle's shell can grow to be over 4 feet long.

6. Octopus

Some larger octopuses have a tentacle span of nearly 30 feet, which is as long as six people standing in a line with their arms stretched out.

7. Blue Whale

The heaviest blue whale ever found was a female weighing 200 tons–as heavy as thirty elephants.

8. Whale Shark

Whale sharks are so big that sometimes they bump into boats in the ocean.

9. Manta Ray

Manta rays can measure 20 feet in width, almost as wide as a swimming pool.